About Starters Facts

This colorful new range of information books encourages young readers to find out things for themselves. The text is graded into three reading levels — red, blue, and green. As well as providing a valuable source of reference, the books encourage further interest in the topic through activities and puzzles.

Accompanying each FACTS book is a STARTERS STORY, which uses the same topic as the starting point for an exciting story.

This book, **Moon,** is linked to a fantasy called **Anna and the Moon Queen.**

Reading Consultants

Betty Root, Tutor-in-charge, Center for the Teaching of Reading, University of Reading.

Geoffrey Ivimey, Senior Lecturer in Child Development, University of London Institute of Education.

Moon

illustrated by

Jill Fenwick

Starters Facts · Green 2

If you look up into the sky, on most nights, you will see the moon. The moon goes around the earth. One side of the moon is lit up by the sun. The other side is always dark. The moon goes around the earth, and the earth goes around the sun.

Once every month, light from the sun shows up all of one side of the moon. We call this a 'full' moon. Two weeks before, sunlight falls on a small part of the moon. The moon then looks thin. The shape that it makes is called a crescent. This is a 'new' moon.

It takes the moon 27 days and 8 hours to go around the earth. Long ago people watched the moon as it went around the earth, and they divided the year up into months. The first calendar was worked out nearly 4,000 years ago in Babylon.

The moon makes changes happen in the sea. Twice a day it pulls the sea a little way toward it, and lets go of it again. The level of the sea rises and falls. These changes are called 'tides'.

People used to think that the moon was a god or goddess. In ancient Egypt the moon god was called Thoth. People thought that he measured out the months and the years. They named the first month of the year after him.

Four hundred years ago a man called Galileo lived in Italy. The telescope had just been invented, and he used it to study the moon and the planets. He discovered that there were mountains on the moon.

Mercury Venus Earth Mars Sun Jupiter

Since Galileo's time, scientists have found out much more about space. The sun, which gives us light and heat, is a star. There are many stars in the sky. The sun has nine planets spinning around it. One of these is the earth.

Saturn   Uranus   Neptune Pluto

All of space is called the universe. Our group of planets is called a solar system. The sun is at its center. The solar system belongs to a great collection of stars and gases called a galaxy. There are many galaxies in the universe.

The moon that goes around the earth is only one of many moons in the solar system. Most of the planets have moons. Our moon is as old as the earth, but it is not made of exactly the same rocks.

All objects in space pull other objects near them. We call this pull 'gravity'. The sun's pull, or gravity, is so strong it keeps all the planets on course. The moon's gravity is weak. If you went there, you would be able to jump high and carry heavy rocks.

For thousands of years people have dreamed about traveling in space. They have looked up into the sky, and wondered what it would be like to stand on the moon. But it is only in the last twenty years that space travel has been possible.

In 1957 a Russian dog called Laika was sent into space in a satellite. In 1961 a Russian man named Yuri Gagarin went up in a rocket called Vostok and made the first spaceflight. When he returned to earth he was a hero.

In 1969 two Americans called Neil Armstrong and Edwin Aldrin became the first people to reach the moon. They set off in a rocket with another astronaut called Michael Collins. When they got near the moon, they traveled around it in their large spacecraft.

Then Neil Armstrong and Edwin Aldrin flew down to the moon's surface in a small spacecraft called the lunar module. They collected dust and rocks to take back to earth, and they set up experiments that would send information back to earth.

The surface of the moon is very
different from the surface of the earth.
Nothing grows there. People used to think that
there was water on the moon. When they
drew maps of the moon, they gave
names like the Sea of Tranquillity
to large parts of it.

But the astronauts found no water. The surface of the moon is dry and dusty. There are many mountains and many deep pits called craters. Some of the craters were made when lumps of rock called meteorites crashed into the moon's surface.

When astronauts land on the moon they may see the earth in the sky. There is no wind on the moon, so everything is completely still. The footprints that the astronauts made will stay there forever, because there is no wind to blow them away.

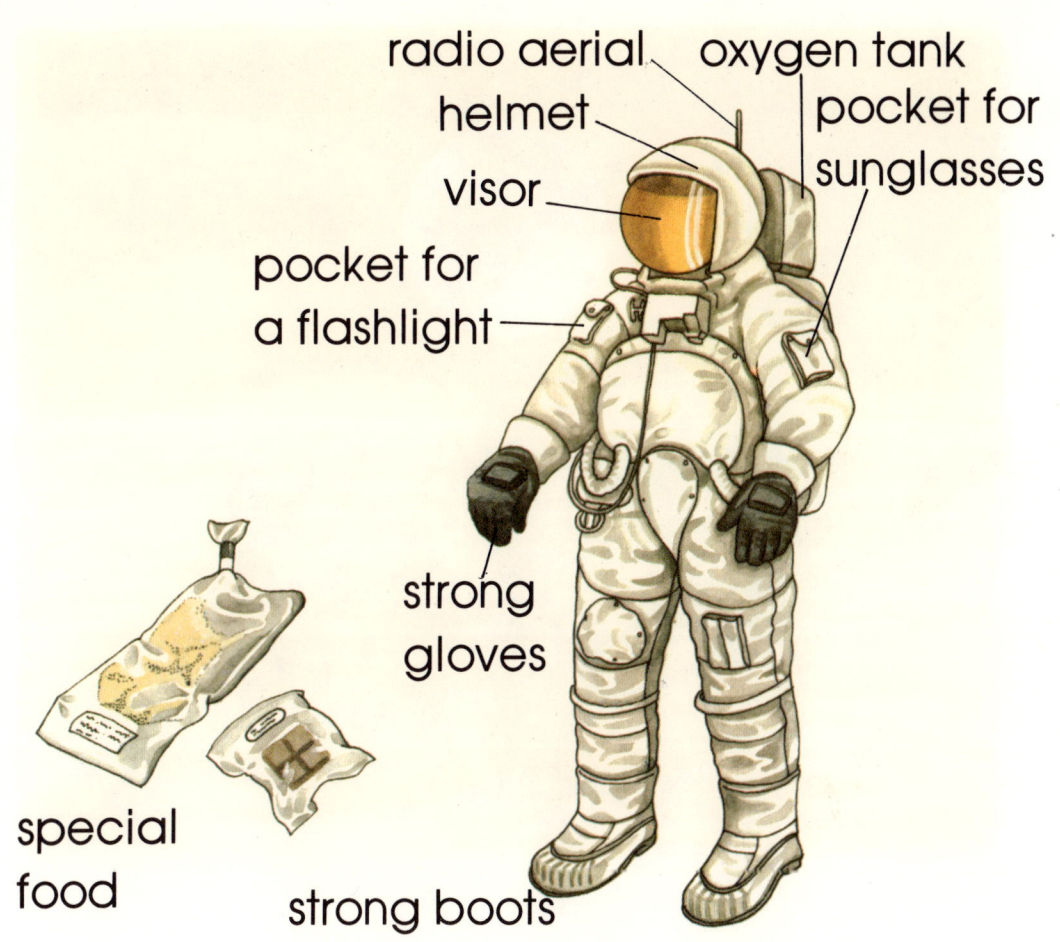

On the moon the days are very hot and the nights are very cold. The astronauts have to wear special suits to protect them from the heat and the cold. There is no air to breathe, so they have to carry tanks of oxygen on their backs.

lunar rover

After Neil Armstrong and Edwin Aldrin went to the moon, other astronauts followed. They took extra equipment with them. Some astronauts used a special car, called a lunar rover, to travel longer distances on the moon.

Getting back to the earth from space is very dangerous. When astronauts come back into the earth's atmosphere, their space capsule gets very hot. The capsule has parachutes fixed to it. These open out, and slow down the capsule, which then lands in the sea.

Even when the astronauts are back on earth, they are not allowed to go home right away. They have to tell scientists all about their spaceflight. The trip to the moon takes only four or five days, but the astronauts have to train for years before they can go.

In the future the moon might be quite crowded. A space village could be built there, for people to stay in when visiting the moon. An observatory might be built, for looking at the earth and the planets, and the sun and stars.

 # Moon Activities

Make you own lunar rover.
You will need 1 large cereal box, 4 round cheese boxes, 1 egg box, 1 pencil, and 1 smaller box. Also aluminum foil, scissors, glue and paper fasteners.

1. Cover all the boxes in aluminum foil.

2. Fix the cheese boxes to the cereal box with paper fasteners.

3. Glue 2 of the egg shapes to the front of the cereal box.

4. Glue the small box on top of the cereal box.

5. Decorate all of the lunar rover.

Moon Quiz

Look back through the book, and see if you can answer these questions.

How often is there a full moon?

What shape does a new moon make?

Who first saw mountains on the moon?

Who were the first 2 men on the moon?

How are craters made?

Moon Puzzle

The lunar rover is lost! The astronaut does not have much air left in his tank! Can you help him find his way back to the lunar module?

Moon Word List

crescent page 3		lunar module page 15	
tides page 5		craters page 17	
telescope page 7		lunar rover page 20	
solar system page 9		parachutes page 21	
rocket page 13		space capsule page 21	

Each information book is linked to a story in the new **Starters** program. Both kinds of book are graded into progressive reading levels — red, blue, and green. Titles in the program include:

Starters Facts
RED 1: Going to the Zoo
RED 2: Birds
RED 3: Clowns
RED 4: Going to the Hospital
RED 5: Going to School

BLUE 1: Space Travel
BLUE 2: Cars
BLUE 3: Dinosaurs
BLUE 4: Christmas
BLUE 5: Trains

GREEN 1: Airport
GREEN 2: Moon
GREEN 3: Forts and Castles
GREEN 4: Stars
GREEN 5: Earth

Starters Stories
RED 1: Zoo for Sale
RED 2: The Birds from Africa
RED 3: Sultan's Elephants
RED 4: Rosie's Hospital Story
RED 5: Danny's Class

BLUE 1: The Space Monster
BLUE 2: The Red Racing Car
BLUE 3: The Dinosaur's Footprint
BLUE 4: Palace of Snow
BLUE 5: Mountain Express

GREEN 1: Flight into Danger
GREEN 2: Anna and the Moon Queen
GREEN 3: The Secret Castle
GREEN 4: The Lost Starship
GREEN 5: Nuka's Tale

First published 1980 by
Macdonald Educational Ltd.,
Holywell House,
Worship Street,
London EC2

© Macdonald Educational Ltd. 1980

ISBN 0-382-06489-5
Published in the United States by
Silver Burdett Company
Morristown, New Jersey
1980 Printing

Library of Congress
Catalog Card No. 80-52523

Editor: Annabel McLaren
Teacher Panel: Susan Alston, Susan Batten, Ann Merriman, Julia Rickell, Gwen Trier
Subject Consultant: Neil Ardley
Production: Rosemary Bishop